# Greater Than a
# Vienna
# Austria

## 50 Travel Tips from a Local

### Melanie Hawthorne

Order Information: To order this title please email lbrenenc@gmail.com or visit GreaterThanATourist.com. A bulk discount can be provided.

Cover Template Creator: Lisa Rusczyk Ed. D. using Canva.
Cover Creator: Lisa Rusczyk Ed. D.
Image: https://pixabay.com/en/panorama-vienna-austria-city-view-427929/

Lock Haven, PA
All rights reserved.
ISBN: 9781549679964

# >TOURIST

Melanie Hawthorne

# BOOK DESCRIPTION

Are you excited about planning your next trip?

Do you want to try something new?

Would you like some guidance from a local?

If you answered yes to any of these questions, then this Greater Than a Tourist book is for you.

Greater than a Tourist – Vienna, Austria by Melanie Hawthorne offers the inside scoop on Vienna. Most travel books tell you how to sightsee. Although there's nothing wrong with that, as a part of the Greater than a Tourist series, this book will give you tips from someone who lives at your next travel destination. In these pages, you'll discover local advice that will help you throughout your trip. Travel like a local. Slow down and get to know the people and the culture of a place. By the time you finish this book, you will be eager and prepared to travel to your next destination.

Melanie Hawthorne

# TABLE OF CONTENTS

12. Try A Foreign Delicacy At The Naschmarkt

13. Feel The Christmas Spirit At A Christmas Market

14. Pet A Dinosaur – Visit The Museum Of Natural History

15. Admire The Lipizzans

16. Soak Up The Atmosphere In The Stadtpark

17. Take Your Dinner For A Spin At The Donauturm

18. Go Toe To Toe With The Creatures Of The Sea

19. See The World's Oldest Purpose Military Museum

20. Celebrate New Year's On The Heldenplatz

21. Go Shopping On The Mariahilfer-Straße

22. Experience A 'True' Austrian Dinner

23. Try Ice Cream For Breakfast

24. Read A Book In The Most Beautiful Library In Town

25. Sip A Cocktail In 'Le Loft'

26. Taste The Eismarillenknödel

27. Take A Dip In The Biggest City-Spa In Europe

28. Admire Snapshots In The Westlicht Gallery

29. See Where Some Of Vienna's Best Are Buried

30. Listen To Viennese Folkmusic

31. Visit A Mall That Spans Three Blocks

32. Look Into The Past In A Former Insane Asylum

33. Admire The Beauty Of Art…With A Twist

34. Dive Into The Minds Of Murderers

35. Discover Your New Favorite Cocktail

36. Try A Pakistani Buffet

37. Keep An Eye Out For Stunning Graffiti

38. Waterski On The Danube

39. Take The Twin City Liner

40. Have Breakfast Above The City

41. Hang Out With Vienna's Punks

42. Dine In The Dark For Charity

43. Hike Through The Lobau

44. Learn The Waltz

45. Rent A Sailboat

46. Get Yourself A Traditional Austrian Outfit

47. Sip Japanese Tea While Petting Cats

48. Have A Pub Crawl Through All 23 Districts

49. Attend A Ball – Life Ball, Opera Ball

50. Run The Vienna City Marathon

Melanie Hawthorne

Our Story

Notes

# DEDICATION

This book is dedicated to my lovely fiancée and the city I was born in. Thank you both for many beautiful years.

**Melanie Hawthorne**

# ABOUT THE AUTHOR

Melanie Hawthorne, née Rittinger, is a writer and author who lives in London. Melanie loves to travel to new places almost as much as she loves to revisit old ones. She grew up in Vienna and only left to pursue her passions – they led her to the UK.

She would love to travel all the way around the world in one trip!

Melanie Hawthorne

HOW TO USE THIS BOOK

The Greater Than a Tourist book series was written by someone who has lived in an area for over three months. The goal of this book is to help travelers either dream or experience different locations by providing opinions from a local. The author has made suggestions based on their own experiences. Please do your own research before traveling to the area in case the suggested places are unavailable.

Melanie Hawthorne

# FROM THE PUBLISHER

Traveling can be one of the most important parts of a person's

life. The anticipation and memories that you have are some of the

best. As a publisher of the Greater Than a Tourist book series, as

well as the popular 50 Things to Know book series, we strive to

help you learn about new places, spark your imagination, and

inspire you. Wherever you are and whatever you do I wish you

safe, fun, and inspiring travel.


Lisa Rusczyk Ed. D.

CZYK Publishing

Melanie Hawthorne

# WELCOME TO &gt; TOURIST

Melanie Hawthorne

# INTRODUCTION

Who doesn't love to travel? Or, if you're stuck at work in an office, who doesn't love to dream about travelling? Vienna is an often forgotten-about travel destination. It's proximity to Bratislava and connection to the Danube make it an ideal pit-stop in any tour around Europe though – and don't be surprised if it entices you to spend your whole holiday there! Combining the charm of its Baroque buildings and coffee-culture atmosphere, it's not hard to see why it's a holiday favorite for many.

If you're a fan of classical music, odds are you've been to Vienna before – that doesn't mean you've seen all it has to offer though…

**Melanie Hawthorne**

# 1. Visit The Oldest Zoo In The World

Vienna is home to the oldest zoo in the world, founded in 1752. Formerly owned by Austria's royal family, the Habsburgs (which will also feature further down in this list), the original cages are still part of the current setup. They are no longer in active use of course, as the conditions the animals were kept in at the time were rather abysmal compared to today's standards.

Now, you can actually enter the old enclosures – they are also outfitted with brass statues of the animals they used to contain. The perfect opportunity for a good photo. The zoo itself is now much, much larger than it was; if you want to visit it all, it'll be a day trip. Alongside the traditional enclosures for animals like lions, giraffes and zebras, there are also opportunities to get up close and personal. Several enclosures actually let you walk through them, and should they choose to, the animals can walk right up to you. Amongst these species are several monkies, butterflies and birds, and you can even enter a

3

bat cave where you will feel the bats fly by at break-neck speed…one might even barrel into you if you move too fast! If the bats are too adventurous for you there's also an aquarium, a rainforest house, a petting zoo, and the most popular attraction: the panda enclosure! Vienna has been one of the only countries to successfully breed pandas in the last few years (other than China of course), and the little ones are always an absolute must-see.

If you're looking to cool off, you can also attend some animal feedings – ask an employee for the schedule, you might be lucky enough to get splashed with some water by a seal at feeding time!

## 2. Visit Vienna's Vineyards

There are over seven square kilometers of vineyards within city limits. You'll find the best quality whites in the 21st district. If you want the full Viennese wine experience you'll have to visit a 'Heuriger', a particular kind of restaurant that will serve

local wines and cold platters. If you're not a wine fan, this could

still be for you: The beer selection is almost as great as the wine

selection, and the designated driver can always indulge in a

glass of homemade fresh apple juice.

A true Heuriger won't serve hot food, only cold platters,

cheese, sausages, and typical Austrian bread and snacks. To

complete your experience, you'll probably also want to indulge

in an Eismarillenknödel – a peachy ice cream delicacy local to

Vienna.

## 3. Enjoy The Sun At The Beach

Vienna in particular, and Austria in general may be

landlocked, but that doesn't mean that you can't take a

proverbial break from your city holiday to put your toes in the

sand. In the middle of the city, the Neue Donau channel is

flanked by beaches – the so called Donauinsel, an island in the

middle of the Danube, is the ideal spot for all sorts of

summertime activities and sports. Most notably though, it

contains various beach and swimming spots.

If that's your crowd, you can even find some nude bathing spots…If it's not, you may want to steer clear of all areas marked FKK on local maps. Along the channel in the inner districts of the city, you can also find some artificial sandy beaches to enjoy a cocktail at. Don't try to swim there though – unless an area is marked, it's probably forbidden…

## 4. Indulge Your Inner Child, Go See The Prater

No town would be complete without an amusement park, but not all can have their own version of Disneyland. Fortunately, Vienna has something that's (almost) better. The Prater.

Located in the 2nd district of the town, it is a combination of a huge green park; ideal for romantic walks and morning runs, and an amusement park. Unlike most, entry is completely free, you only pay to get on rides. Many of them are family-owned and have been run by the vendors for years and years – you'll get an honest view at some of Vienna's culture. From wild rides to little stalls you can find something for everyone here. At a fairly affordable 3-5€ each, you'll be able to enjoy a few rides.

Just be sure to always watch the ride you're about to get on – some of them are wilder than you think! Now, if you take a look at some of the postcards for sale in the area, you'll notice they all have something in common – the Riesenrad. It's a giant ferris wheel, lifting you a solid 65 meters off the ground. It's quite popular so you'll have to queue for a while, but the views and photo opportunities from the wooden gondolas are to die for.

For those with a fear of heights: Take photos from below or visit the attached museum instead.

## 5. Do Some Cardio – Rent A Bike

Vienna has huge stretches of bike paths making it one of the safest towns in Europe to cycle through. There's plenty to see too – a thousand kilometers of bike paths will let you visit every part of town. If you didn't bring your own bike that's ok, there's both private and city-owned rental services. Citybike is one of the best on offer. You can register online or buy a card with some credit on it at a tourist info center, and off you go.

There are over 60 rental stations to choose from, and you can pick up and drop off bikes 24/7 at your convenience. If you return a bike within the hour of renting it, it's even free – if you keep it for longer, a charge may apply.

Good thing is, you can return your bike to any of the points, which means you can give the tube and tram lines a skip and do some exercise while exploring the city. If you get lost and see some other bikers, don't be shy about asking for help – the cycling community in Vienna is one of the friendliest you'll find. They're sure to be able to point you in the right direction, and you may even find some buddies to have a pint with on the way.

# 6. Have A Coffee

The coffeehouses in Vienna are very well-known. The coffee itself isn't just what it's about though. Sure, there's plenty of good brews around, but it's about the experience as a whole. The traditional Viennese coffee house visit will happen in the late morning of a Saturday or Sunday (any other day is fine too of course), a local paper which will usually be provided by the coffeehouse on request, and the coffee itself.

The most common thing to order would be a 'Melange', a dark coffee with a little bit of milk. If that doesn't appeal, Espresso, or a Caffé Latte are also perfectly acceptable choices. You will want to order a sweet snack with it. The menu will list your choices here. Servers usually speak at least a little English, so if you're not sure what to get, don't worry about asking for help.

Quite often this will be a social activity, so other visitors might have a chat if you're alone. If you don't speak German, don't worry about it though. This part of the experience is absolutely optional. If you want to, you can also have a pint of beer afterwards, as many coffeehouses will serve it. For the best experience you will want to pick a location with a view – be it the Stadtpark or even a particularly busy street for you to watch.

## 7. Snack On A Continental Breakfast

The continental breakfast is something you can get in many places across Europe, but in Vienna you will often find it combined with the Baroque charm unique to the city. Pick a location like the Hotel Sacher or the Grand Hotel, but be prepared to pay for it. The location matters as much as the actual food. You'll be having some bread rolls with jam, cheese and some ham, all ingredients on the side. While the conventional choice of beverage is coffee or tea, in winter, a hot chocolate is also quite a good choice.

Don't be afraid to Instagram your breakfast – just be sure to also include some of the lovely location you're having it at!

## 8. Visit A District Museum

Vienna is made up of 23 districts. They are loosely centered around the 'middle' one, which is the 1$^{st}$. The outer ones are a little more scrambled, with the 10$^{th}$ being next to the 23$^{rd}$ for example.

They all have something in common though – they have a very rich and often unique history. Most of them have permanent local museums. They tend to be rather small but are filled with the most wonderful things, stories and even recommendations for places to visit in each district.

As an example, the 22$^{nd}$ district has a partnership with the 22$^{nd}$ district of Tokyo – Japan has gifted them several original Japanese cherry trees that are now planted in a little orchard in that district. It's free and publically accessible, so if you are lucky enough to go there during spring, you should keep an eye out for the pink and white blossoms. Other districts have similar unique spots. The museum in the 1$^{st}$ district has some very detailed fables and legends local to Vienna. Most of them were

11

created or 'took place' before the city expanded to its outer

districts, so there are many fancy stories and legends around.

That museum also features some beautiful drawings and

illustrations. You might just be inspired to visit some of the

spots of those stories – don't worry, most of them are in walking

distance.

As mentioned, almost all districts have museums like this,

so ask a local about the nearest one – in whatever district you

may end up in.

## 9. Inspect The Original Furniture Collection Of The Habsburgs

Nestled away in the center of the city, surrounded by tourist

traps, is a much lesser known museum. It features the original

furniture used and owned by the Austrian royal family. If you've

already seen the Hofburg, you may have found it to be mostly

empty and devoid of furniture – this is where it ended up.

Set up like a mock-warehouse, you'll be able to admire the fancy chairs, cupboards and beds that once outfitted the palace. You can even try out a few of them. Spoilers: Some of them are prettier than they are comfortable.

Many have stories attached to them too. For example Empress Sissi, one of the most popular and beautiful royals, had a peculiar habit: She believed that sleeping on pillows would crook your back and so, every night, she would throw all her pillows from her bed. She would then demand the maids put them all back, and she would do it all over again.

Some of the old beds were also not designed to lay down in – they would sit, and sleep with their backs to the headboards. Sounds pretty uncomfortable, but that was tradition. If you're not interested in furniture, there are two more museums in the same building – one detailing the making of Papyrus, and one the language Esperanto. It is not a 'natural' language spoken anywhere, but rather artificially designed by language experts to be easy to learn and universally useable. You won't find many of Vienna's people that speak it, but it is still an interesting spot away

13

from the beaten tourist tracks.

## 10. Ride The Ring-Tram

Vienna features plenty of tram lines – several dozen. With only 5 tube tracks spanning the city, trams are often the way to travel. If you explore the city you'll likely ride them a lot anyway – but this particular tram is different.

It is a round-trip starting at Schwedenplatz tube station. It costs a little more than your everyday-tram trip, however you get given a pair of headphones – they plug into the seat in front of you. You then get to pick an audio-track in your language before the trip starts. As you travel the Ringstraße, the track will point out interesting buildings and locations around.

From a planetarium to the main university building and parts of the Danube, there is plenty to see. If you like any of the places that you see, you can switch to a normal tram line and see most of them up close.

If you aren't sure what you want to do after the tram trip,

the tube station in question – Schwedenplatz – is home to some of the most exquisite ice cream shops in town. Take your pick and try some of the more adventurous flavors. There are often specials that you can only get for a certain amount of time. A definite Instagram favorite!

*"Dream on, but don't imagine they'll all come true. When will you realize... Vienna waits for you." -Billy Joel*

## 11. Taste Zotter Chocolate Or Visit A Chocolate Museum

Vienna and Austria are well known for their sweets and snacks. Chocolate is no exception. One brand, Zotter, actually has its' factory in another part of Austria – where everything is sourced and produced as locally as possible. They don't do your everyday standard chocolate either – they're all about unique

15

tastes and experimental combinations. From fish (yes really) to cheese to jalapenos, they probably have a flavor for it.

You'll be able to buy their chocolates in most mom and pop sweet shops, possibly even in supermarkets – don't expect any of the more experimental flavors though.

If just a taste isn't enough, in the 23$^{rd}$ district hides a particular gem – a chocolate museum. From a general history of chocolate, through the process of making it, you'll get to see all the steps up close. You'll even get to watch some of the workers make the actual chocolate – and as a special treat, you can try as many as you like. In the obligatory shop, you'll be able to buy something called 'Bruch'. This is chocolate that was damaged during the making, tastes absolutely fine, but doesn't look quite right.

It's incredibly cheap and a lovely treat to bring home as a keepsake. Or to eat on the spot. In fact, that is my recommendation.

## 12. Try A Foreign Delicacy At The Naschmarkt

The Naschmarkt (translated, Snack Market) is an absolute gem hidden in the middle of Vienna. Placed alongside the U4 tube line, it is easily accessible and quite close to other interesting places.

As for what it actually is – it's a combination made up partially of a flea market, and partially of an open food market. You won't find any supermarkets here, however the stalls and shops have their own lovely charm you won't be able to forget easily.

Much of the food available isn't Austrian at all – instead you will find fresh food from all over the world. Whether you crave exotic fruit, spices, or innovative snacks – you won't go hungry here.

Several times a week, the market is also extended with another section, consisting entirely of an antique and flea market. You won't find kids trying to sell bicycles though –

instead, most of the wares on offer are antiques and art. You'll definitely be able to make a bargain here. Don't be surprised if a shopkeeper won't sell you an item without telling you it's story first – you pay for the history as much as for the item itself.

When you've had enough of the bustle of the eternally-busy market, you can find several unique coffee shops scattered along the sides of it. Should you be interested, there are also a good two dozen Asian supermarkets along the Naschmarkt itself. They are much quieter, and if you are thinking of bringing home some exotic spices, this is the way to go.

# 13. Feel The Christmas Spirit At A Christmas Market

These are a seasonal occurrence of course. Opening mid-November, and usually staying open until early February, you'll love the Christmas markets. Whether you're window-shopping or gift-buying, the wooden stands and festive decorations are sure to get you excited for Christmas.

Vienna has several markets – usually up to a dozen – that are open during this time period. They tend to be quite different from each other, so you'll get a unique experience every time. The most popular and well known one is the one in front of the Rathaus – the city hall – which is mostly made of traditional seasonal food stalls and lots and lots of kitschy gifts.

Another one in front of the Karlskirche, is mostly made up of woodwork and handicrafts; featuring unique handcrafted items and gifts…and of course some seasonal food.

One of the lesser known markets is placed in between two museums – the Naturhistorisches Museum and the Kunsthistorisches Museum. Fairly close to the Ringstraße, you'll have an easy time finding this one. In addition to its lovely seasonal foods (you may be beginning to notice a theme here), you'll find many handcrafted and natural gifts. From woodcarvings and handmade candles to hand-stuffed air freshener bags, you'll be able to find something truly unique

19

here.

Be sure to try a mug of Glühwein or Punsch while you're there. Not only does it get served in an adorable porcelain cup you get to keep (or return for a small discount), but it also tastes divine. Whichever market you choose, it's sure to get you into a festive mood.

## 14. Pet A Dinosaur – Visit The Museum Of Natural History

Vienna's museum of natural history is one of the most well-known and popular ones around the world. If you truly want to see all it has to offer, you'll have to spend several days here.

In addition to an extensive (and interactive!) dinosaur section, it also features just about everything else you can think of – be it minerals, aquatic life, or a stuffed elephant. There is even a small indoor Planetarium. For a small extra fee, you'll be able to watch the stars, volcanoes, or any other kind of show you may be interested in. Be careful though, the tickets sell out quite fast. If you need one you can ask for an audio-guide in your language, so you can really keep up with what's going on.

One of the lovely things about this museum is, that almost everything is interactive. While you won't be allowed to touch any of the animal exhibits (animatronic dinosaurs being the exception), many of the exhibit pieces invite you to swipe, touch and poke your way around them. Don't be shy – touching allowed!

## 15. Admire The Lipizzans

Nestled in the center of Vienna, close to the Hofburg palace, is the Spanish Riding School. It is a traditional Baroque style building with stables right inside the building itself.

This school only has one breed of horses – the much admired Lipizzans. White by default, they also have some of the incredibly rare brown and black horses, and quite often have foals to view.

21

Every morning their horses are taken out for a trot in the courtyard, which is open to the public. The school also has guided tours during which you'll be able to see and pet some of the horses up close. If that still isn't enough for you, once a week, they also put on fantastic dressage shows – truly an experience not to be missed.

## 16. Soak Up The Atmosphere In The Stadtpark

The Stadtpark is one of the most iconic pieces of land in Vienna. Although not the biggest park in town it stretches all the way from the 1st into the 3rd district. It is home to lots of statues of famous Austrian musicians – so many in fact, that it is called the musical park by some, and the park of statues by others. It holds the record for the most statues in any park in Vienna.

If you are a fan of classical music, you will definitely want to visit and stroll through here. Its most famous monument, the golden Johann Strauss statue can be seen from its main entrance, as well as several passing tram lines and busses. So even if you are only passing by, be sure to take a snapshot of it.

The park is a very popular location for picnics, running and yoga; so if you are looking for an opportunity to get some morning exercise, this is the place to be. The park is also home to the 'Kursalon' a spa-like building that, back in the 1800's was famed for its local mineral water. It now holds a café and restaurant in it, as well as several baroque and renaissance paintings and decorations.

## 17. Take Your Dinner For A Spin At The Donauturm

The Donauturm, or Danube Tower, is located in the 22nd district of Vienna, in the middle of what I (and many others) consider to be the city's most beautiful park. It is very close to the Danube and even a public swimming area.

23

The park features several exceptional flower gardens, a Chinese pavilion, and even a beekeeping area. As for the tower itself, it stands at 252 metres tall, and ranks among the 75 highest towers in the world. If you are scared of heights, you will probably want to give this one a skip.

For a little history: It was built and opened in 1964, and achieved its goal of being the tallest structure in the entire country. Its most interesting features are the viewing platform and the spinning restaurant.

The viewing platform is the highest publically accessible part of the tower, and gives a beautiful 360° view of Vienna and its surrounding areas. The restaurant is one level below it. The tables are placed alongside the glass exterior of the tower, allowing for an amazing view as you dine. The floor actually spins as you eat – although very slowly, it takes nearly an hour for the restaurant to complete a full circle – meaning you get to see just about everything.

The food itself is lovely too – traditional Austrian meals as well as some modern cuisine, and an excellent wine collection. Be careful if you go to the bathrooms though – they do not rotate, so your table will have moved by the time you get back.

If you're worried about finding it again, ask one of the staff for help. Don't worry – it happens often!

## 18. Go Toe To Toe With The Creatures Of The Sea

Placed in the 6<sup>th</sup> district, this aquarium is overlooked by visitors far too often. Calling it an aquarium does not quite do it justice – it is also part museum and features creatures like crocodiles, sharks and even a few birds.

Most of its tanks are of the seawater variety – the biggest tank is inhabited by black-tip reef sharks. From shrimp to alligators, you'll be able to admire most sea-creatures here. The aquarium also has a museum attachment in which it showcases information about creatures that cannot be kept in an aquarium, such as giant jellyfish or deep-sea squids.

An interesting feature: The rubble and rocks at the bottom of most of aquariums is local – it is recycled and prepared rubble left over from World War 2. The building itself is a former flak tower, standing at 75 meters tall.

## 19. See The World's Oldest Purpose Military Museum

Hidden away in the 3rd district is another one of Vienna's lesser known museums. It is the oldest military museum in the world and its exhibits feature weapons, armor, tanks, airplanes, uniforms, flags, paintings, medals and badges of honor, photographs, battleship models, and documents.

As a special treat there is also the Panzergarten – a garden filled with tanks and a few full-sized military airplanes. Very close to the museum is an excellent restaurant – the Arsenalstuben. It features similar decor as the museum, and is a great place to have lunch after viewing the Heeresgeschichtliches Museum or HGM, as it is called.

## 20. Celebrate New Year's On The Heldenplatz

Vienna hosts a series of spectacular events each year on the Heldenplatz (hero square) each year. Check online before you visit to see what's going on at that time. Two of the most iconic festivals you'll see are the New Year's celebrations and the Independence Day festivities.

For New Year's each year, a spectacular firework show is launched after midnight, and this is the place you want to be to see it. It is visible from other places as well, but this is truly center stage.

The square will be filled by celebrating people, so don't be surprised if you're offered a glass of champagne by a stranger – this is as social an activity as it gets. Just before the new year, there will be a countdown of the last 10 seconds before midnight, at which point a Viennese waltz will play – dancing optional, but encouraged.

The independence day celebration takes place on the 26th of

October. Here, the Austrian military hosts a parade, exhibition and show in the square.

You'll have the opportunity to climb into a real tank, or try your hand at shooting a high precision sniper gun – not with real ammunition of course. You'll be able to admire officials of all ranks in their gala uniforms. Don't be shy about asking to take a picture, as most of them will be more than happy to.

While you are there, don't forget to try some Gulasch, an Austrian variation of a Hungarian dish. It is considered the 'standard' food for the military, much like donuts are often jokingly referred to as the police's favorite food.

A stew-like dish, you'll be served by the actual cooks that supply the troops with food while they are stationed for duty.

*"Dear Vienna, are you singing? Dear Vienna, are you swinging?" – Owl City*

## 21. Go Shopping On The Mariahilfer-Straße

This street is one of the most popular shopping locations in the city. It spans several districts and is chock full with all kinds of shopping opportunities.

You can find any kind of shop on this street. Grocery shops, food shops, electronics, books, fashion, adult toys, furniture, even the odd car dealership. The street is almost 2km long, and actually connects the 1st district with the 14th. While not the longest street altogether, it is the longest shopping street.

If you are looking exclusively for designer and branded things, you'll be better off on another street – the Kärntner Straße, but for general shopping, this is where you want to visit. If you want to stop for a snack, find a kebab shop. There are several along the way, keep an eye out for ones that belong to the 'Turkis' chain – they are particularly delicious.

If you are looking for something more off the beaten track, walk down some of the side streets, to find local shops with character. From a small Irish pub to several shops selling handmade clothing and jewelry, you won't be disappointed.

If you are into board games or tabletop games, one of Vienna's most favourite game shop can be found here as well – Damage Unlimited. It also sells a variety of medieval weaponry and costumes, so you may want to have a look.

## 22. Experience A 'True' Austrian Dinner

There are many traditional Austrian restaurants in Vienna. From the 'Heuriger' to 5-star cuisine, you can find anything you'd like. But, if you are looking for a truly traditional experience, you'll want to visit the Schweizerhaus. Although its name translates to Swiss House, it is the most complete experience you'll find. It is near the Prater and impossible to miss.

It has its own version of a drive-through, albeit in a pedestrian zone, and both cyclists and pedestrians can stop there to pick up snacks. One of their best ones is the Kartoffelpuffer, a flat potato patty grilled and served with plenty of garlic. Following closely behind is their chips (for the British: their crisps) which are made of an entire potato that is sliced very thinly into a spiral, and then deep fried. Although the spiral will break, they are fresh, and absolutely lovely.

If you want a sit-down meal, simply ask a waiter for a seat. You'll be given a menu, asked what you'd like to drink (careful, you'll likely encounter a strong accent and not too much English here), and then get to choose from several warm meals. Pick anything you like, or ask the waiter for advice and go with the daily special.

Whatever you pick, you are sure to experience one of the most iconic dining experiences in town, fully including the rustic charm of a decades old restaurant.

## 23. Try Ice Cream For Breakfast

Very close to the center of the city is one of its best ice cream shops and cafes. Zanoni & Zanoni, commonly called the Zanoni, serves some of the best ice cream you will find in town. Unfortunately, they don't usually carry it in winter, so mind the season when you visit.

Their ice cream is made fresh on site every morning,  and some of their more popular flavors easily sell out by early afternoon, so be sure to visit by lunchtime.

In addition to their ice cream selection, they also offer a lovely selection of breakfast sandwiches and dishes. They're made fresh every day, and they have many organic, vegetarian and even vegan options; so everyone will be able to find something they'll enjoy here.

## 24. Read A Book In The Most Beautiful Library In Town

Whether you love books or not, visiting the National-Bibliothek is definitely something you should try to plan into your trip. Like much of Vienna's architecture, it is a beautiful baroque building, with bookcases spanning several floors. Many of the reading halls are two floors high, and the upper shelves can only be accessed via several ladders and thin balconies respectively.

Should you want a book from that high up, you'll have to ask staff for help – they are closed to the public. However, much of the rest of the library is accessible.

If you're interested, there is a literary-themed tour you can take part in, but you can also simply choose a book and read it. You'll be able to find both local and international authors and books here. It is the biggest library in Austria, and it has a very extensive collection of poems and contemporary pieces. If you are interested in art, several beautiful paintings pre-dating the world wars are hung in the halls of the library…just be sure to keep quiet while there!

## 25. Sip A Cocktail In 'Le Loft'

The bar Le Loft is on the 18th floor of a 5-star hotel – the Sofitel. It's a skybar, so it's located on the very top floor. You'll have one of the most stunning views of the city from here, and if you're lucky enough to catch the sunset, you're guaranteed a breathtaking view.

As if that wasn't enough, there is another feature that makes this tip an exceptional one, and that's the roof. It's a piece of artwork in and of itself – made by Pipilotti Rist, it is essentially a giant painting.

If you don't want to visit the somewhat pricy bar, you can easily see the ceiling from the ground, as it is quite spectacular. It has backlighting too, so don't worry about visiting after dark to take some photos.

## 26. Taste The Eismarillenknödel

This is an ice cream treat that is only manufactured by one ice cream shop in all of Austria. It's called Tichy, and is located in the 10th district. During the times they make the Eismarillenknödel, there will often be queues around several blocks, and more often than not, they will be sold out within hours.

As for what it actually is…at the center is a home-made thick peach puree, surrounded by specially made vanilla ice-cream, and covered in a shell of breading made out of vanilla sponge cake.

Be on the lookout for special editions – every year they offer some unique alternative versions; for example, one with a raspberry center and chocolate cake breading. You'll not miss the advertisements around town either – they are colorful and spread out everywhere during summer. You'll even find hints as to what flavors are on offer that year!

## 27. Take A Dip In The Biggest City-Spa In Europe

The Vienna City Spa, or Therme Wien is one of the most amazing and yet absolutely affordable spas in Austria. It consists of several indoor and outdoor pools, a sauna area, and several other attractions.

So whether you're the type that likes to relax in cool water in the dark, or would rather spend the day sliding down a variety of slides, this spa has you covered.

There's a kids area, a sports pool and even some water aerobics classes all included in the entry price. The only thing you'd have to pay extra for are massages and other services like that. You'll be given a wristband to access your locker as well as 'book' additional services should you want to.

You'll pay when you leave, so you really want to make the most of your time there. A special tip: There is an outdoor pool that plays underwater music. Simply submerge your ears and you'll be able to hear – it's quite a unique experience.

## 28. Admire Snapshots In The Westlicht Gallery

The Westlicht Gallery is unique amongst the many (many, many!) art galleries in Vienna. The only thing featured here are photographs – photographs of anything and everything.

You'll find them displayed in somewhat unconventional methods though. Some of them are printed, others are, for example, projected onto different surfaces. Some are even interactive and will give you the opportunity to learn more about photography.

You'll find opportunities to get more intimately familiar with cameras, even getting an chance to arrange and take your own photo in the studio.

So, if you have an interest in photography, or even just need something to fill a slow afternoon; you'll find this gallery, and it's connected camera museum, well worth your time.

## 29. See Where Some Of Vienna's Best Are Buried

Vienna's Central Cemetery is a bit of an oddball among the attractions the city has to offer. It is the biggest cemetery in town, and also placed quite centrally. Not everyone can be buried there either, you have to either already own a plot, or 'earn' one by merit.

Buried here are some of Austria's most iconic artists, musicians and politicians. The cemetery itself has been featured in lots of popular songs and writings.

Despite being a place of remembrance and paying respects, it is publically accessible and has many crypts, statues and monuments that are very popular with visitors. Mozart, Salieri, Brahms, Strauss, all have monuments here.

It is one of the largest cemeteries in the world, and in fact has its own joke: Half the size of Zurich, but twice as much fun. It refers to a somewhat joking rivalry between Austria and Switzerland, but it also isn't entirely inaccurate – the cemetery is so large it has its own bus line traversing it, the 106 route.

Another local joke refers to 'taking the 71'. The 71 is a tram line that ends at the gates of this cemetery. Unsurprisingly, it's a joke about someone dying and ending up in a cemetery.

## 30. Listen To Viennese Folkmusic

Vienna is perhaps most known for its classical music, but the so called Volksmusik is more than worth a listen. This is something you can easily do while travelling or even relaxing in your hotel at night, so be sure to give some of the more popular artists a try.

The 'Austria 3' are an incredibly popular trio of individual singers that would occasionally make music together – often for charity. The three men it consists of, Georg Danzer, Reinhard Fendrich and Wolfgang Ambros are largely considered to have coined this genre. If you want to get a feeling for Austria in general and Vienna in particular, they are where you want to start.

If folk isn't for you, there is another Austria-specific genre, called Austropop. It's a little more modern and upbeat than the

39

more traditional folk music. Some of the most notable bands here include STS and EAV. The latter's music is satirical, as you will notice from watching their music videos. Despite this, they are still very popular. If you are trying to learn a little German, you may find EAV and STS to be very helpful, as they enunciate very clearly.

If you are hunting for a humorous gift or keepsake, you might want to look into finding one of their CDs to take with you.

If you are looking for the most successful Austrian artist, that would be Falco. He was the first ever to top the Billboard charts with an Austrian-German song, something that has not been done since. The song is called 'Rock me, Amadeus'.

*"Es war in Wien, war Vienna*

*Wo er alles tat" – Falco (about Mozart)*

## 31. Visit A Mall That Spans Three Blocks

By far the biggest shopping mall in Vienna, the Donauzentrum has evolved from a 'normal' shopping center, to an urban entertainment center. In addition to well over 250 shops, located in 3 buildings connected by bridges, it has several entertainment areas.

The mall is 3 floors high and has steadily been expanded upon, until it's reached its current record size. Built right next to a large traffic junction, the three blocks are connected via bridges and walkways that cross the roads below.

Alongside the shops, there are also numerous restaurants, bars, coffee shops and also one of Vienna's biggest cinemas.

In the downstairs areas, there are several bowling lanes and some pool tables, as well as a small casino – you'll be able to keep yourself entertained all day.

This shopping center is in the 22nd district, and easily reachable via various methods of public transport. If you visit during winter, located opposite of the mall is the Albert Schultz

Eishalle, an ice rink with a capacity for 7000 people – it is however, only open during winter season.

If you are interested in ice hockey, you might be able to watch a game or training, and if not, the rink is often open to the public, so you'll be able to skate yourself.

## 32. Look Into The Past In A Former Insane Asylum

The so called Narrenturm, or Fool's Tower, is the oldest mental institution in Europe. Built in the early 1700s, it was in use for only a few decades, before being turned into a museum. It is home to one of the oldest lightning rods in the world, which can be inspected on site. The museum inside it now shows both the conditions former patients lived under, and also the kinds of 'treatments' they'd be subjected to. At 5 stories tall, one of the most distinguishing features of this building is its shape – it is completely circular. This has spawned many local jokes.; for example, referring to the building as a 'Gugelhupf' (a kind of circular sponge cake).

## 33. Admire The Beauty Of Art...With A Twist

The Fälschermuseum in the 3<sup>rd</sup> district is a unique museum
– its art is anything but. Its collection consists of fakes and
forgeries of famous art pieces, and is dedicated to some of the
best forgers in the world.

From paintings to pages from Hitler's diary, everything in
the museum has been proven to be counterfeit. This museum is
the only one of its kind in all of Europe and aims to teach it's
visitors more about the different kinds of fakes, the difference
between a copy and a forgery, and even shows how to spot
certain types of counterfeiting.

Opposite of this museum is something else worth visiting –
the Hundertwasserhaus. It was designed by Friedensreich
Hundertwasser, an expressionist. It's now an apartment
complex, but the facade has not lost its splendor. It plays with
optical illusion and colors – you'll definitely want to take some
selfies here.

## 34. Dive Into The Minds Of Murderers

The Kriminalmuseum or criminal museum is dedicated to all things murderous, such as historically important killers and victims from Austria. From serial killers to crimes of passion, they deal with the macabre.

A small warning: Most of the exhibits and information is in German, but some have English translations as well. There's still plenty to look at in regards to torture devices, skulls and skeletons as well as other paraphernalia, but the explanations are in predominantly in German.

It is not an expensive museum and the ambience is great, so you may still want to visit if you are in the area.

If you speak German (or have a good translation app/local friend), you'll definitely enjoy this museum. The building it is housed in is one of the oldest in town, and the historic feel of it really helps build the ambience of mystery, crime and murder.

## 35. Discover Your New Favorite Cocktail

Hidden away in the 20th district, is the bar 'The Sign'. It is easily one of the best cocktail bars in town if not the country, and yet not that well-known.

Or, to be more precise, the locals keep it to themselves. If you are looking for an amazing cocktail experience, this is the place to go. You have two options: Sit down at a table and a waiter will bring you a menu, from which you can pick your drink, or, sit at the bar and tell the barkeep you aren't sure what you would like.

You'll be asked a few questions, such as your favorite alcohol or fruit, and the barkeeper will pick and make you a drink. If you get the chance, you will definitely want to give this a try – the staff's intuition is all but never wrong!

Don't be surprised if you see them use some…unconventional ingredients either – from raw eggs to pickled scorpions you'll see all sorts of things. Don't worry though – you won't get a cocktail like that without the barkeep making sure you're okay with it. If you're not sure what sort of thing to ask for, try a personal favorite: Ask the barkeep for a pear and vanilla cocktail.

## 36. Try A Pakistani Buffet

As far from traditional, or indeed, Austrian food as it gets, Der Wiener Divan is incredibly popular with locals, especially students. The Pakistani restaurant is in the 9th district and fairly close to several university campuses.

What makes it so unique is that it is not only a buffet-style, all you can eat deal, but that you get to name your own price. Whether you want to pay 1€ or 20€, it's up to you.

The owners have said in many interviews that their strategy pays off – often people pay a little more than they would have paid á la carte, and this helps them provide low priced foods for those who cannot afford more.

Everything they offer is completely organic, and there are many vegetarian and vegan options – you'll definitely not go hungry here.

There's more than food on offer as well – if you are interested, you can ask the owner for permission to play one of the sets of traditional drums around the restaurant. Once a month, locals will even have a little jam session with these instruments. Should you meet the owner, you may want to ask him about the story of the restaurant – it's quite an adventurous one!

## 37. Keep An Eye Out For Stunning Graffiti

Vienna and art are inseparable, that's undeniable. On top of the more conventional forms, you'll also be able to spot another kind: Graffiti.

Not the kind that kids use to deface shop windows with rude little pictures, but proper artwork. Oftentimes these are maintained by either the artist or the city. A good example here is one that even has its own name: The Frog of Vienna. It's located in the 20th district, along the channel. If you can't find it, ask a local – just about everyone would know where it is. It would be impossible to list all the locations this type of art can be found, however if you want a place to start, look along the Danube.

The various channels, bridges and even buildings near the water are a prime location for epic artwork. While generally a crime, the city has given permission for certain areas to be sprayed, making it less an act of vandalism, and more an expression of modern art.

In fact, you'll be hard-pressed to find a  bridge with no graffiti under or around it at all – some of them even depend on the level of the water, being only partially visible when the tide is high, and completely exposed when there is less water.

Happy Hunting!

## 38. Waterski On The Danube

Whether you're interested in trying it or just watching, this one is a must-visit during summer. 'Wake Up' the restaurant in question is called. It is located in the 22nd district – but only just, as it is on the bank of the Danube.

Combined with the restaurant is a wakeboard lift. As you

eat (or have a beer at the bar below the restaurant) you'll be able to watch the wake-boarders and water-skiers try their best.

The restaurant is open all year round but the lift is not, so if you want to watch this spectacle, be sure to check if they are really open beforehand. If not, the food is pretty good, so you may want to visit anyway.

If you get really lucky you'll be able to watch some of the top Austrian athletes train there. Several times a month, the lift will be closed to the public for them to practice. Either way you might be lucky enough to watch people pull off some cool tricks… or just stay on the board, which is hard enough to do!

## 39. Take The Twin City Liner

The twin city liner is aptly named as it connects two Cities – Vienna and Bratislava. In just over an hour, this boat can take you from one city to the other.

So, if you are looking for an excuse to take a boat on the Danube, but don't want to pay hundreds for a boat-cruise, this is a great alternative. You'll be able to catch a boat in the morning and another back in the evening, just be sure not to miss the trip back or you'll be stranded.

What you want to do in Bratislava is up to you – shopping, sightseeing or a pub crawl. You'll find that quite a lot of souvenirs are a little cheaper to get in Bratislava than they are in Vienna, so this might be a great opportunity to do some inexpensive shopping.

Be sure to take plenty of photos on both of your boat trips as the views are magnificent. Often the crew will also be around for a chat, so don't hesitate to ask them questions about the trip.

## 40. Have Breakfast Above The City

In the 7$^{th}$ district, very close to Vienna's biggest concert and event hall the Stadthalle, is another one of its biggest libraries. While not nearly as big as the National library, this one is one of the largest lending libraries.

More interestingly, on top of said library is a restaurant with a rooftop terrace. There are two ways to get up to the restaurant – via an indoors lift, or via many (many, many) stairs.

Once at the top, you'll find the vegetarian restaurant Oben, or Above, and the name certainly fits. The restaurant itself is encased in glass walls with outside seating in good weather. You'll be able to enjoy a delicious and quiet breakfast while watching the people below bustle to work. Beneath the library and restaurant is a tube station of the line U6, so if you enjoy people-watching, this is the place to be.

Tip: Although it's a vegetarian restaurant, if you look carefully on the menu, you'll find a few meat options!

*Haben Sie Wien schon bei Nacht*

*gesehen? Haben Sie das schon erlebt?*

*(Have you seen Vienna at night?*

*Have you already experienced this?)*

*– Reinhard Fendrich*

## 41. Hang Out With Vienna's Punks

If you are interested in Vienna's small but thriving punk scene, you have a few options: The tube station Museumsquartier is a popular hangout for punks. You won't be able to miss them – big colorful hair, ripped clothing and usually with some music playing.

Not too far from this spot is the Arena, in the 3rd district. This space hosts several different events, concerts and art installations, most of which are Punk or Rock themed. You should check in advance what sort of events are being held and when.

If you are here during summer, you might also want to drop by to check out the open air cinema that is hosted here every year. On a 400m² lawn, you'll be able to enjoy a movie in a new perspective.

## 42. Dine In The Dark For Charity

In Vienna's Vier Sinne, or Four Senses, you get to dine in the dark. With the exception of the entrance way and the washrooms, everything is pitch-black. From when you enter, you will be led through the dark by your waiter, and seated.

You don't get to pick your food either – while you do get the opportunity to let the staff know about any allergies, the food is pre-selected. Who could read the menu without light anyway?

The dinner consists of a starter, a soup, a main and a dessert. In addition to the delicious food you'll encounter the obvious difficulty of eating without seeing – don't wear your Sunday best here, as you might spill something.

All the waiters are visually impaired, most of them severely so, and the restaurant itself is partnered with a charity to raise awareness for the issues that sight-impaired people face in their daily lives.

You'll find the staff there to be very understanding and helpful – if you want to visit the bathrooms, a waiter will have to lead you there and most likely back.

As you leave, you are shown the dishes that you had, so, if you tried to guess what it was, you'll be able to find out whether you were correct or not.

## 43. Hike Through The Lobau

The Lobau is part of a large stretch of National Park. So huge in fact, that it stretches all the way into Slovakia. Over 9.300 hectares, this park is mostly forest.

It is accessible to the public, however certain areas are sectioned off for the protection of the animals living there. These animals include species like wild boars, foxes, various kinds of deer and more.

If you're interested in any of them, there are usually tours early in the morning and late at night. Your guide will try to show you around and even give you an opportunity to take photos of these animals. If that's not what you're after though, you have lots of other options – several of the natural lakes are very popular with locals for a dip in summer, and the wide meadows are often used for BBQs and picnics. Be careful though, as BBQ-ing is only allowed in a few restricted zones and you will get fined if you caught anywhere else.

Throughout the park you will find lots of opportunities to follow set hiking and biking paths, as well as informational signs on points of interest in the area.

Be sure to wear hiking shoes though, as the ground isn't always even!

## 44. Learn The Waltz

The Viennese Waltz is perhaps the most well-known of its kind, and you'll hear it at practically every event with classical music you'll see in Vienna.

The dance however, is far less known. It used to be taught in schools during gym class, however that hasn't been the case for years. It's a fairly simple dance though, and can be learned in just a few hours.

As such, there are quite a lot of 'drop-in' dance schools in central Vienna, such as the Tanzschule Rueff. You can drop in when they have a class and join – you'll have the basics down in no time.

If you don't have a partner, don't worry about it – in that sort of class you'll easily pair up with someone else, which will even give you the opportunity to chat to a local.

Alles Walzer!

## 45. Rent A Sailboat

Austria is landlocked, so you won't get the chance to sail on the open seas, but the Danube is nothing to scoff at! Whether you get a small one-person boat, or one for several people, sailing down the Danube is great fun.

If you are so inclined, you can try windsurfing as well – the winds aren't always strong enough though, so keep an eye out for the weather. If need be, you can always row a boat, but with a surfboard you might get stranded.

There are several surf and sailing rentals along the Danube, especially in the 22nd district, so head there if you want to give it a try. Don't worry though, if you have no sailing experience there are plenty of paddleboats available. Or alternatively, you could take a class learning how to sail – they usually take a half day, and you'll learn useful knots and interesting bits about the local waters. Be careful though, don't swim in areas with boats as that can be dangerous!

## 46. Get Yourself A Traditional Austrian Outfit

You've probably seen them, at least in pictures: The Trachten. Traditional Austrian Trachten are somewhat different from the German or Polish ones you may have seen before, though more in the decoration than in cut.

For the gents it's the traditional Lederhosen with suspenders, a white shirt and a leather hat with a pheasant

57

feather (if we are being technical). For the ladies it's two part dress – a very low cut white blouse underneath and the actual dress on top. Sometimes the apron part is sown on, sometimes it comes extra – either way it makes for a pretty unique outfit.

While you won't exactly find this style of clothing in the nearest H&M, you'll definitely be able to find the type of store that does sell it. Almost every decent sized mall will have them, and they usually come in a variety of colors and cuts. If you're not sure what will suit you, don't worry and ask an employee for help. If they suggest an unusual color, don't be too surprised either, as bright yellows and oranges and even pinks aren't unusual to see. So, whether you're shopping for a keepsake or your next Halloween costume, a traditional Austrian Trachten-do is sure to turn heads.

## 47. Sip Japanese Tea While Petting Cats

The Neko café isn't original to Vienna, as they first became a trend in Japan. However, the one in Vienna is still worth a visit as it is a quiet spot to relax and have a cup of tea.

Located in the first district, this café is populated with rescued cats. Most of them are very happy to be petted, held or have their bellies rubbed while you enjoy a newspaper or a small snack.

You can even ask for cat treats, but not all cats are necessarily allowed them, so please be careful before you feed any of them. The idea behind the café is that people who visit can adopt the cats after a certain time of getting to know them. That means that you won't always meet the same cats. The café adopts new ones from shelters all the time.

Keeping in tradition with the original neko cafés, you'll mostly find Japanese teas and sweets here, such as Mochi and teacakes. Enjoy the purrfect afternoon here!

## 48. Have A Pub Crawl Through All 23 Districts

Vienna's 23 districts aren't as big – or indeed as far apart, as one would assume. A pub crawl through all 23 of them is

59

absolutely doable, and quite enjoyable too.

If you think that's too much, restrict it to the inner 10 districts. You'll probably need a 'Beisl' map, as pubs are called, so be sure to plan out where you want to go ahead of time – asking drunk strangers for their best pub recommendation could be a little risky.

It'd be a lot safer to ask a barkeep – odds are, they know the area you're in, and they'll be able to give you better recommendations. If you're looking for a place to start, consider the Kern Beisl or the Bastei-Beisl. Both are lovely for a dinner and a beer, before you move on to the other districts.

If you make it all the way to the 22nd district, you will definitely want to stop bei 'Selitsch', it's one of the best ones in town. Prost!

## 49. Attend A Ball – Life Ball, Opera Ball

Attending a ball in Vienna is quite a big deal – they don't take place year round, and instead are confined to a certain season, referred to as 'ball season'. Check before you visit what balls are planned, and pick one you'd like to attend.

When you've found one, be sure to purchase the tickets well in advance as they are prone to selling out fairly quickly. Some of the most popular balls include the Opera Ball, which is the event of the year; the incredibly opulent and magical Life Ball, and others like the confectioners ball, where everything is themed to be sweet and sugary!

You'll need the appropriate attire to attend each event, otherwise you'll be turned away at the door. For women this is a ball gown or other formal elegant dress, and for men it's a smoking jacket with a tie/bowtie.

The exception here is the Life Ball. It is held each year to raise AIDS awareness, and has a theme, such as fire or water. Instead of traditional ball clothing, this event calls for costumes. If you want, you can still wear your normal ball gown or suit, but if you truly want to go for the whole experience, you'll want to find (possibly even rent!) a costume.

There are of course a dozen more balls each season, so if the glitz and glamour of the big ones is more than you're looking for, choose a smaller one instead.

## 50. Run The Vienna City Marathon

The Vienna City Marathon takes place every year. The admission fees go towards charity every time; so whether you actually run or just attend, you're supporting a good cause. If you want to attend but aren't much of a runner, don't worry – walking, jogging and even one-legged hopping are allowed.

The marathon itself is only part of a larger event. For those who don't want to run, there are lots of stands and attractions put next to the running track. These include sponsored food booths, memorabilia shops, and the occasional music stage.

There are also presenters that will, via speaker, occasionally announce a particular runner, such as Cheryl Hile, who, in 2017, ran the marathon despite suffering from Multiple Sclerosis.

If you're in Vienna around the time of the marathon, you won't be able to miss it – the advertisements are rather impossible to overlook.

# Top Reasons to Book This Trip

- **Unique Charm**: A mix of old and new.

- **Austrian Food**: Don't miss out on the Schnitzel.

- **Baroque Glamour**: A rich heritage of tradition.

# > TOURIST

## GREATER THAN A TOURIST

Visit GreaterThanATourist.com
http://GreaterThanATourist.com

Sign up for the Greater Than a Tourist Newsletter
http://eepurl.com/cxspyf

Follow us on Facebook:
https://www.facebook.com/GreaterThanATourist

Follow us on Pinterest:
http://pinterest.com/GreaterThanATourist

Follow us on Instagram:
http://Instagram.com/GreaterThanATourist

65

Melanie Hawthorne

# > TOURIST

## GREATER THAN A TOURIST

Please leave your honest review of this book on Amazon and Goodreads. Thank you.

We appreciate your positive and negative feedback as we try to provide tourist guidance in their next trip from a local.

# > TOURIST

## GREATER THAN A TOURIST

### Our Story

Traveling is a passion of the "Greater than a Tourist" series creator. Lisa studied abroad in college, and for their honeymoon Lisa and her husband toured Europe. During her travels to Malta, an older man tried to give her some advice based on his own experience living on the island since he was a young boy. She was not sure if she should talk to the stranger but was interested in his advice. When traveling to some places she was wary to talk to locals because she was afraid that they weren't being genuine. Through her travels, Lisa learned how much locals had to share with tourists. Lisa created the "Greater Than a Tourist" book series to help connect people with locals. A topic that locals are very passionate about sharing.

Melanie Hawthorne

# > TOURIST

## GREATER THAN A TOURIST

### Notes

Printed in Poland
by Amazon Fulfillment
Poland Sp. z o.o., Wrocław

19232644R00052